Origami

Everything You Need to Know About Origami from Beginner to Expert

Sandra Gifford

Sandra Gifford

Sandra Gifford

Table of Contents

Introduction

Welcome to the world of origami, also known as paper folding. It is a rich, unique and illustrious trade with a long and somewhat mysterious history practiced by people of all ages around the world. Origami has seen the rise, fall, and rise again of its popularity throughout the ages. But because of its strong foundation built over a number of generations, the art and practice of origami continues to develop to this day.

Once you step into the multidimensional realm of this fun hobby, it may be easy enough to get lost in the folds of all the variety it has to offer. Developed throughout time from a few key locations on the globe, what we see today is a mixture of various styles that offer different methods of folding according to your particular taste. They range from the simple and entertaining to the meticulously detailed and complex, from a one-size-shapes-all to the modular construction of individual component folded pieces, interlocking into each other to make a grand design. Techniques can be seen from being highly geometric to the more organic and natural, producing hard and jutting borders or smooth curves for a soft touch.

You will find much more to come within this book as you read on. Learn a brief history about the art, what materials are available to you to get started or improve and advance your current technique, as well as a number of common folds that are shared among many origami patterns. These folds will help familiarize you with common base constructions and develop a more fluid approach to those tricky twists and turns in the more advanced designs.

If there is one thing to know about origami before you get started and one thing to take away from the practice of it at any level, it is that origami in and of itself develops the virtue of patience. The paper is thin, the steps are outlined in order, and just to wrap one's head around how the importance of one particular fold is going to affect the overall creation will begin to see your mind unfurling in new perspectives. Therefore, the rewards of taking up origami are not only fulfilling on a basic entertainment level, they provide existential value for years to come. So step in, unwind, and come get a further glimpse into this delicately mesmerizing world of paper art.

Thank you for purchasing this book.

Sandra Gifford

Origami Origins

There is a bit of speculation when it comes to deciphering the exact origins of this paper folding art in both place and time. Because it happened such a long time ago and paper does not preserve well, especially in early times, many researchers confer to the origins of paper itself. Although many people are aware of the ancient Egyptians having invented the first material to function as paper, known as papyrus, the earliest remnants of paper as we know it today is widely attributed to Cai Lun (also seen as Ts'ai Lun) of China as its inventor in the first century A.D.

Five hundred years later in the sixth century, Buddhist monks travelling the Silk Road brought paper to Japan. The ingenuity of Japanese minds indeed made several improvements to the sturdiness and pliability of paper over the years, adding quality and manufacturability so that it was accessible to the general public. Up until that time paper had been a luxurious item because of the rarity of resources in combination with the arduous process to make it. Thus, it is difficult to know whether paper folding actually began in China or Japan.

While China has been seen to have its own style of paper folding, known as zhezhi, the art form did not gain nearly as much popularity in its culture as the origami art in Japan during early times. Japan is often attributed as the culture bearer of origami because from early on, particular designs were embedded in its religious and ceremonial practices. For example, during Shinto weddings, paper butterflies decorated sake bottles for the new couple. These early representations of origami had a particular design designated for the female, known as "Mecho" and "Ocho" for the male.

Furthermore, the Japanese etiquette for gift giving followed a specific tradition of attaching different types of origami embellishments depending upon the nature of the gift: "origami Tsuki" was a particular type of folded paper that represented a certificate of authenticity, "Noshi" adorned gifts as additional mark of good fortune, and "Tustsumi" was formally used for gift wrapping, representing sincerity by their modest design.

Between the history of Chinese and Japanese paper folding, the Chinese style has been particularly noted for its practical designs of its inanimate objects such boxes for holding small edible treats, boats, and hats or helmets. The Japanese style is best known for the more organic designs of flowers and animals. Paper folding in Europe understood thus far is believed to have been introduced by the Moors coming from what is known as the Middle Eastern area between Europe and Asia today, although historians cannot be sure if it was a separate discovery than that of the Far East cultures, or if it was knowledge further acquired and passed on via the Silk Road. Regardless, the European style of paper folding is quite different than its Asian relations, being more precise and geometric in design than the "judgment folds" that allowed Japanese practitioners to fold designs at angles according to their preferences.

As is currently known, the first actual recorded depiction of folded paper art occurring in the form of the classical origami boat was not seen until centuries later in the 1490 printed book "De Sphaera Mundi" (On the Sphere of the World) by Johannes de Sacrobosco of Italy. There is some debate among historians as to whether the boats in this book are actually references of origami or the Chinese form of zhezhi, but it is fairly apparent that the illustrations are closely related to the paper folded models. Further evidence of early paper folding is referenced to kimonos, the traditional style of clothing in Japan, of the late 1600s which depicted prints of the famous origami cranes as well several types of folded boats on them.

Close to the turn of the 18th century, the world saw the first published book on origami titled "Senbazuru Orikata" (How to Fold a Thousand Cranes). The title of this book makes a reference to the faith-based practice in Japan of folding one thousand cranes within a day as a type of prayer to help heal Sadako Sasaki, who was terminally ill after being exposed to the atomic bomb radiation of Hiroshima. This practice can be seen done among classes of school children as a tribute to her, spending an entire day of folding cranes for the beloved member of their community.

Although Sadako did not survive, before she died she wished for peace around the world and suffering to end. The practice of folding one thousand cranes today is now said to be a way to fulfill one's desire in their heart of hearts. Just as with any type of prayer, this practice may find success in accordance with the Laws of Attraction, which deem that the repeated effort of a singular concentrated intention facilitates bringing about the realization of that intention. And as you become familiar with the practice of origami, the concentration and patience it requires nurtures the grounds for any such intention. Consider the phrase, "you can do anything that you put your mind to."

As for the book itself, "Senbazuru Orikata" was predominantly an introductory effort toward diagramed origami instruction, since there were no steps in folding these designs to attain the finished product; the pages instead only depicted the finished product and left readers scratching their heads as to the process of how to reproduce it.

During the 19th century, the popularity of traditional origami saw growth by being taught in kindergarten and elementary school classes, most notably in Germany through the influence of Friedrich Fröbel, but also in Japan as a teaching tool during the Meiji period (1868 – 1912). Up until this time throughout history, origami instruction was largely an oral tradition passed down through the generations. The publication of the book "The Art of Chinese Paper Folding" by Maying Soong in 1948 was a great contribution to help spread the practice and also made a distinction between the Chinese and Japanese styles, as previously described.

It was not until 1954 that Akira Yoshizawa and Sam Randlett produced the first comprehensive, step-by-step diagram system for learning how to fold origami designs. These diagrams are the basis for most all origami instructional books published today, utilizing a system of squares, dashed lines, and various arrows to guide the aspiring origami student through turning a flat sheet of square paper into any number of completed designs at any skill level. Robert Harbin is credited to later teaming up with Sam Randlett to improve upon the basic system that Akira Yoshizawa invented. This simplistic format is formally known as the Yoshizawa-Randlett system, used around the world today.

What is known as modular origami was brought into popularity by a group of Chinese refugees who had stowed away on the ship "Golden Venture" and were imprisoned upon arrival to the United States in 1993. Using a combination of papier-mâché (toilet paper) and Chinese modular paper folding (via any material they could find, such as magazine pages), these refugees constructed larger recognizable designs by interlinking the modules together and gave them to people helping the refugees at the time, who then sold these models through fund raisers. Their efforts caught media attention, which thereby trail blazed the awareness of this new method to be implemented across the U.S.

As it has been introduced to you from the beginning of this book, methodologies and types of origami are constantly being developed and evolved. You will come to learn about these various types in the next chapter. Currently there are over 50 international organizations and societies specifically dedicated to the art and practice of origami, as well as many more national subgroups that meet together at annual grand conventions. From China, Japan, Israel and numerous European countries to Africa, Argentina, Brazil, and the United States among others, there are hundreds of thousands of people who gather together to celebrate the craft. If you are so inclined to join one of these groups or attend one of their conventions, you can easily find lists and meeting dates of the organizations with some light research online.

Types of Origami

How would you like to create a paper boat that actually floats on water without sinking, or a variety of airplanes that can do a number of tricks and flight patterns through the air? Are you particularly fond of decorating your home or office with paper flowers and animals, or have children, neighbors, friends or relatives who may be entertained by them and like to receive them as gifts? How about making a paper evergreen tree for Christmas, three-dimensional dreidels for Hanukkah, or other outstanding designs as side projects to sell? With origami, you can even make intricate geometrical placemats, jewelry, and art pieces that can be laminated or bronzed and metal plated (yes, it has been done) to be preserved and enjoyed to your delight and that of others for years to come!

The following are examples of the virtually endless possibilities for various origami types. These are not particular individual figures, mind you; they are various methods of origami that you can make any number of designs from to explore, develop and diversify your craft. There are so many different origami styles and methods in fact that you will not find all of them described here, however these are among the most popular and conventional types. There are people in the world so well versed in these various styles that some of the most interesting, intricate, and prominent creations have earned the honor of being placed on display at museum exhibitions around the world!

Traditional

This type of origami derives its style from the historical roots of the designs that originated the practice. They entail some of the more basic forms that upon completion usually end up lying flat, being two-dimensional, although there are patterns that are pseudo-two-dimensional (they stand up but still have predominantly flat features), and three-dimensional.

Models that particularly fall under this category are ones such as the Japanese "Mesho," "Ocho," "Noshi" and "Tustsumi" decorative adornments for gift giving. Other examples are the classic origami boat that can also open from the bottom and double as a hat that you may be familiar with, boxes, samurai helmets, simple flowers, animals (sometimes just the head, but also ones with the entire body), as well as the ever-popular crane. These designs are particularly noted for their simplicity and usually only require a handful of steps to complete, ideal for the beginner.

Modern

There is a library of designs that fall under this category. Sometimes modern designs of origami patterns will be confused or associated with the Traditional types, and this is logical since many of them are derived or adapted from the Traditional models. However, with a little exploration and discretion, you will come to find that the modern style of origami is quite extensive and can reach much further in complexity than that of its Traditional cousin. It is a great avenue for the beginner and intermediate person to expand their skills, solidify their knowledge of folds and improve their completion time.

Modern designs of origami include a wide array of animals, boats, flowers, trees (such as palm trees and Christmas trees!), famous buildings, holiday symbols, and pretty much any other object or iconic figure you can think of. There are several variations of patterns for creating hearts for Valentine's day, Santas for Christmas, pumpkins, witches, ghosts, etc. for Halloween, and Turkeys for Thanksgiving. There is even a niche entirely dedicated to Star Wars – origami Yodas, Darth Vaders, X-wing fighters, you name it.

While Traditional origami may produce the designs of common animals like the cat and various birds (which look more like a collection of triangles), they require more imagination to envision what the intended representation is. Modern origami styles have applied the imagination right into the creation of the design, producing life-like two and three-dimensional models of rhinoceroses, pandas and koalas clinging to bamboo poles, horses in action poses, dragons of both the European and Chinese variety with wings or full-fledged scale bodies and flowing whiskers; hopefully you are getting the idea here. The flowers of Modern design pay tribute to many species, although one of the most beautiful and popular designs is the (new) Kawasaki swirl rose. Sounds tempting to take on, doesn't it? It's something to work up to – that one is challenging for intermediate origami enthusiasts.

Action

Although this type of origami could technically fall under the Modern style classification, the Action style of origami garners enough patterns and brass to earn its own established group. Action origami can actually incorporate other styles as well, but its predominant feature is that these completed designs do not stop at the end of folding; they are interactive, too.

Some common models of the Action variety include pinwheels, Chinese throwing stars, airplanes, flying birds, jumping frogs, and three-dimensional sailboats and motorboats that actually float on water without falling apart (depending on the type of paper you use). Other patterns that can practically be considered Action types are unique envelopes, boxes for holding candy, treats, and lightweight gifts, as well as Chinese lanterns.

Golden Venture

The Golden Venture style of origami refers to that particular method of folding modules popularized by the Chinese refugees in 1993. The modules themselves have a precise pattern that, when completed, resemble three-dimensional triangles with a tab and slot feature so that multiple modules can be interconnected together. Once you have folded several modules, you can begin interlocking them like building blocks to shape larger designs that resemble any number of objects you wish.

Modular

The concept of Modular origami is very similar to the Golden Venture method however the modules under this category are not limited to the precise triangular Golden Venture pattern. They can be folded into a number of different geometric polygons and designs with the same kind of interlocking feature. You can find patterns that use one principle module design or others that incorporate two to three different modules to build a variety of attractive three-dimensional shapes, usually geometric themselves. Imagine also that because you are creating individual modules to assemble together, you can use a variety of different colored paper to add intrigue and appeal to the overall design.

Examples of the forms created from assembling these modules include tetrahedrons, dodecahedrons, lattice-looking animals, starbursts and so on. They make great decorative pieces for the office desks, shelves, or ceilings to hang from for kids, college students, architects, technical designers, or anyone who is spatially drawn to three-dimensional art.

Wet Folding

This style has been a recent and interesting adaptation to the conventional Modern designs of paper folding. It has become so diversified by pursuant origami architects that Wet Folding has shot off virtually into its own art form. Through the creative results of the most inventive artisans, some among the origami community have been left to speculate if Wet Folding should still be considered origami or verily classified as *paper sculpting*.

Even from a modestly experienced origami folder's point of view, Wet Folding is a relatively easy and unique transition from Modern construction, although it does take a different approach and practice. Essentially, you would be folding the same pattern as you would from one of the Modern designs. The difference is that you will start out with the paper being wet. The main change in approach here is that you must fold quickly because you do not want the paper to dry before you are finished. Having said that, it is beneficial to be intimately familiar with the particular design you are going for in a dry run before attempting the wet version.

You do not want the paper to be dripping wet, so the use of a spray bottle to sufficiently dampen it is enough. Also, to ensure that your creation does not begin falling apart in the midst of the process you will want to seek out a thicker grade of paper; there is a specific type called "elephant hide" that is commonly used with Wet Folding, although this style is not so popular as to easily find this type of paper in stores, so you will most likely have the best luck getting resources online.

The visual difference of Wet Folding is really appealing. If you thought that Modern origami did a good job of creating three-dimensional figures relative to the Traditional designs, Wet Folding brings these creations to life even more by softening and rounding out the folds, creases and edges so that the overall figure looks more natural. Even if this style does not sounds like something you would likely experiment with, it is well worth your time to cruise the internet for images of Wet Folding origami, especially the masks.

Tessellation

Oh, the origami Tessellations – phew! If a picture is worth a thousand words, absorbing the intricacies of Tessellation origami will leave you speechless. That is, of course, unless you go after attempting it, in which case you may find yourself singing a string of obscenities that you didn't know you could be so colorful with. To be straightforward, Tessellations are more advanced designs that require the utmost patience, a keen eye for detail and the softest meticulous touch. There are varying levels of skill patterns that range from the pleasantly simplistic to the "Woah..." And if you are serious about your origami, completing a Tessellation can be the most rewarding style to take on as well.

Their appearance looks similar to a quilt of interweaving design patterns, creating layers of different mesmerizing shapes that overlap each other. You are not interlacing strips of paper together though; you are working with one sheet of paper. Speaking of the paper, the Tessellation origami style involves multitudes of tiny folds, so finding a material that is thin to accommodate the tight overlapping shapes yet very durable to sustain the multiple folds is ideal. It is recommended to begin with a good quality photocopier paper or art type of paper because you don't want to spend money on specialized paper that you are more prone to make mistakes on. Once you have become comfortable with the Tessellation style and feel confident to go for a showpiece, you can find specialized paper such as Tant, Lokta, or Stardream online to buy.

Completed Tessellations are so pleasing to look at and they can serve functional uses too! The paper can be laminated or sealed in epoxy so that you can use them for placemats, coasters, trivets and more if you can imagine it. There are varying sizes of paper to use, so depending on your choice, you can cut a completed Tessellation into modulated pieces according to the pattern design and your preference, poke holes in them and seal them to use as jewelry like earrings, pendants, necklaces, attach them as a crown piece to a ring, create pins or brooches and more still. It may even be worth your while to explore the possibilities of metal plating them, just be advised that this will take some research and caution if you attempt it yourself. You may find luck in finding another party to do it for you.

Dollar Bill

Can you spare a dollar? How about turning it into a valuable origami piece? There are entire books written especially for Dollar Bill origami, believe it or not, and the number of imaginative designs is entirely inspirational. This type of origami is doubly unique because most conventional origami patterns call for a square sheet of paper to begin with, while Dollar Bill origami has obviously made great use of the rectangle.

The types of designs that can be generated from a simple dollar bill include mini T-shirts (some with collars and ties), scorpions, elephants, the Star of David, a heart that can snugly fit a quarter inside its center, a flowered ring embellishment that can securely hold a penny, butterflies, a professional camera complete with lens, a toilet bowl and yes, even a whole series of Star Wars figures including a realistic-looking Yoda and the Millennium Falcon. If you're willing to entertain yourself with a fiver or a tenner, you can always learn to fold up Abraham Lincoln's head into sporting a sideways baseball hat or dress up Alexander Hamilton in a sombrero.

As mentioned before, there is an array of origami styles out there to explore; more than can fit neatly in this book, and at least one that will inspire your paper folding skills to take shape. With the size of each fresh piece of paper starting out, your ultimate creation will be considerably smaller, so you can imagine the size of the origami figures that are created from folding money.

This brings us to two points: one is the additional miniature world of tiny origami that begins with square paper 1 to 2 inches in length (and some even just 1 cm in length, designed by the author of several origami books, Joseph Wu); the second point is that the more complex design you are going for or the more basic your skill level, the easier it will be for you to start out with larger sheets of paper when practicing. Want to know more? Find out in the following chapter on origami tools, paper, and types of folds.

Sandra Gifford

Tools to Use, Paper of Choice and Types of Folds

This chapter is dedicated to the basic elements of the art of origami. Essentially you will find that all you really need when it comes to paper folding are two crucial components: your hands and a piece of paper. You can virtually use any type of paper for origami and your wrists are kind enough to carry your hands with you wherever you go. Accordingly this is what makes the art form so fun and adaptable because you can do it on the spot in nearly any environment.

Newspaper, notebook paper, magazine pages, flyers, business cards, computer paper, cardstock, and even food wrappers make for suitable origami materials. As you get further involved however, you might like to invest in materials that are specifically suited to varying origami needs. These materials depend on the complexity of your design pattern, what style of origami you are using, and the overall appearance of how you want your finished product to look.

For example, more complex patterns will call for a lighter-weight of paper due to the increased number of folds and overlapping that you will be executing since a thicker paper will make the process difficult to impossible otherwise. While being thin or lightweight, the paper used with complex patterns also needs to be sturdy. The basic principle behind this is that the more folds you make and more detail you get into with your design, the more that the fibers of the paper break down and become weak. You want to avoid having your finished product revealing unattractive tears and rips at the creases because the paper could not sustain.

Heavier and simpler types of paper are more forgiving for beginner and intermediate skill levels when mistake correction is necessary. It will allow you to "erase" a misaligned crease and provide room for experimentation. Under each skill level described below, you will find suggestions for appropriate types of paper to use and more from which to explore with design creation and appearance.

You will also see a number of tools that you can use along with the design process that will help you increase your speed, finesse the trickier techniques, and add value to your completed pieces. These tools will be outlined according to the appropriate skill level and techniques you will encounter therein, although their use is certainly not limited to any particular skill level.

Along with the types of paper and tools outlined, there will be folding techniques aptly suited for the design patterns typically used in each skill level. These folds are cumulative, adding to your origami toolbox as you develop your craft. Basically, the intermediate and advanced levels are still going to use the simple valley and mountain folds that are standard even at a beginner level. Along the way you will be presented with suggestions to help enhance your overall creations and elevate your craft to a polished degree and marketable trade quality. So then, let's get into it.

Ease into Beginning

The beginner level of origami art usually refers to people who have never attempted it before, tried it a few times a long while ago or people who practice somewhat but feel hesitant to try new patterns for lack of being able to work through anything that may be too complex. The best styles to work with here are the simple designs of Traditional origami as well as the most basic models of Modern origami that have been derived from Traditional designs.

Paper

The great thing about the practice and experimental stages really at any level is the versatility of material available to you. Fortunately we are not living in the times of the early centuries when paper was limited and considered a luxury. It still pays to save money, so for practicing purposes it is a good idea to reuse anything that is disposable. Reach out for any loose form of paper that you don't have another use for. Grab old flyers, advertisements, newspaper pages, magazines, bills you don't need anymore (talk about turning lemons into lemonade), computer paper, etc.

You will need a relatively perfect square sheet of paper to begin with, and yet most of these free-floating resources are rectangular. How do you convert them? Easily. Simply take one corner of the shorter edge of the paper and fold it diagonally so that the short edge meets up evenly with the long edge. You will have a little of the long edge of the paper left over, basically what appears to be another rectangular piece.

Fold this rectangular strip right over the edge you have created with the diagonally folded (now triangular) side and make a crease that is flush with the triangles edge. Unfold this new crease and cut along it using scissors to trim the rectangular piece off. Unfold the diagonal, triangular piece and there you have it – a perfect square! You could of course always make use of a ruler to measure out your original rectangular paper for a perfect square, but this method will save you time and the bother of looking for one.

When you feel like you have gotten the folds down and are ready for some good looking pieces with a nice kind of paper, you can do a quick search to order online for "origami paper" or "washi," the basic style of Japanese origami paper. You can usually find quality origami paper at your local craft store also in packages of anywhere from 20 to 100 sheets and possibly more at prices of ten to five dollars or less, which proves to be a fairly inexpensive hobby.

The basic style of origami paper usually comes in three different sizes of three, five, and seven inches. The most common are the five inch squares. This origami paper has a solid color on one side, offered in every color of the rainbow as well as brown and black, and white on the other side, which is considered to be the back of the paper. When working with this paper, the instructions will depend on the particular design you are working with, but more often than not you will want to begin with the white side up. The way that the common patterns follow to construct the origami base folds, the color side will end up being on the outside this way.

There are also paper varieties offered that have designed prints on one side and white on the back (this is the "washi," with common Japanese nature art as the prints) as well as dual colored paper (a different color on each side) known as duo paper that looks great for patterns that have some of the back side naturally showing when the figure is finished. A few examples of this are a red side/green sided paper for making an origami strawberry with green leaves at the top, or a samurai helmet that ends up showing the back of the paper for the highlighted trimming of the helmet.

Tools

Really the only tools that you need at the beginning stage are a good pair of hands with fingers that are willing to improve in dexterity. You will want to develop the feel for shaping the creases and folds of the paper, lining up edges and points, and working the paper around in your hands without anything else to focus on. This will really help you create a firm connection between the paper, the pattern and yourself. Pressing down on the paper over a hard surface with your fingers will make a sufficient crease in the types of paper mentioned above. You can also choose to use your fingernail, just note that this will make a more permanent crease.

Folds

There are a few tips for overall folding that will make your experience much easier and give you something to aim for. Many times, step by step instructions of origami patterns will have you fold one corner of the paper to another, an edge to an edge, or an edge to some crease you have already made, known as a pre-crease. These types of alignments reflect the geometric perfection developed from the European style that has been blended in with other cultural influences that has shaped Modern origami to what it is. These alignments are extremely helpful when following instructions that may appear unclear, as well as for helping to execute a perfect design and understanding the nature of origami at large. By understanding its nature further, you are also advancing your skills to be able to take on more challenging patterns.

Therefore, when you see such instructional folds and ever find yourself a bit confused, know that more often than not you should be looking for an edge or pre-crease to line up your folding edge with. Once you have lined them up, hold the paper firmly on that line with one hand and softly round the fold that you're making down with a finger before creasing it. This is the most assured way to get an accurate fold every time, and if your aligning edge slips, you can realign it without having to erase a rushed crease. Remember that origami involves patience, so enjoy the process and go slowly at first as you watch your design develop. With time and practice, your improving skills and knowledge will automatically increase the speed of your folding process as a byproduct.

In terms of instructional design recognition, when following steps for folding origami you should know or it should already be apparent that the solid lines in the diagram represent the edges of the paper. There are two basic folds to know at the beginner level and two basic action diagrams to be aware of when following the instructions in a manual:

Valley fold – This is when you will bend the paper toward you so that from the side you are working with face up, if you open the fold back up you will have an inward crease, looking like a valley. It is often represented by a uniform dashed line going along where the crease will occur.

Another symbol will show a single arrow with a solid or filled head pointing in the direction that the fold should go. These two symbols are usually shown together, and the diagram in the following step will depict how your paper should look with that fold.

Mountain fold – This is when you will bend the paper away from you so that the folded part of the face-up side you are working with will now be facing down toward the surface you are working on. If you were to unfold this crease again keeping the side you started with face-up, you would see an outward crease resembling a mountain. It is often represented by an alternating dot-dash or dot-dot-dashed line where the crease will be. This line is often accompanied with an arrow that has a hollow or outlined head pointing in the direction that the fold should go. Just the same as valley fold, or any fold for that matter, the diagram in the following step will show what the paper should look like with the work you have just done.

Fold and unfold – This is an action in making either a valley or mountain fold depicted by an arrow arching one way, reaching a point (the other side of the fold), and then arching back with the arrow head shown on the arc back. The dashed or dot-dashed line will tell you whether it is supposed to be a valley or mountain fold. Just as the name suggests, this action symbol is telling you to make a fold and crease it at that particular line, then unfold the paper again; do not keep it folded. The intention here is to make a substantial crease, known as a pre-crease, which is often used later on in the pattern to make further folds easier to do, acting kind of like a guideline. You will see an example of this in the petal fold.

Turn over and invisible line – The turn over action symbol is represented by an arrow that has a loop in the middle, telling you to turn the piece over so that the side that was face-up is now facedown. The invisible line is not always depicted in instructional diagrams, but when it is it's shown as a dotted line to represent the hidden solid edge of a fold when the paper is turned over. For example if you had an existing valley fold so that there were some solid lines inside the square diagram representing the folded paper edges and then you were shown to turn the paper over so that your valley fold is now face-down, those solid lines inside would now appear as a dotted line on the turned over diagram.

Level up and Develop Intermediately

The intermediate level of paper folding refers to people who have had experience with the basic designs, know their mountain and valley folds front and back and have little to no trouble reading step by step instructions, understanding what is being asked of them. This skill level sees people having mastered the basic patterns of Traditional origami and find them easy, ready to move on to something more challenging. Does that mean that you are ready to take on your first scaled Koi fish, simple Tessellation, or three-dimensional praying mantis? Perhaps soon Grasshopper san, not too far down the road.

The intermediate level sees and enjoys a wide range of skill level demands from various patterns, some more basic and others feeling close to the advanced level. This range offers a great setting for exploring hundreds of step by step design patterns, many of which can be found online for free, although buying a design book is always an enriching investment that keeps giving back when you have found one with numerous designs that appeal to you. All of these patterns of varying degrees of skill in the intermediate stage will keep you busy making lots of improvements, really immersing yourself in the origami world and getting familiar with common folds and repeating base patterns. The themes here are to dive deep and diversify; you will soon become a seasoned origami whiz.

Paper

You can always stick with the solid-colored paper described in the basic set, although now is the time to really get out there and discover, so why not try something new? The range of origami types of paper are as diversified as are the pattern skills at the intermediate level, so you have many options to choose from. These papers differ in thickness, material, texture, shape, and print.

There are many different kinds of prints for the same kind of basic origami paper, or standard washi. Some of these include chiyogami, which has traditional Japanese art of flowers and nature printed on it, tie dye designs, animal prints, etc. When browsing through washi and chiyogami paper types, know that they vary in weight and texture, as they are made from a range of plant fibers. You will find some that are soft and slightly fuzzy with a stiff, cloth-like fibered back to them.

These thicker grades of paper are well worth the finished product, but there are some things that are helpful to know when working with them. They are going to cause the folds you make a bit more difficult to firmly crease, and thereafter the creases will be a bit harder to see. Also, more complex designs will prove an additional challenge working with thicker or heavier paper because of all the multiple folds and layers you are creating with them. The more layers you have, the harder it will be to fold in the later stages and maintain a well-defined, clean-looking piece.

It will depend on the type of pattern you choose to employ, and they will specifically call for it, but there are options available for rectangular-shaped paper (please recall the Dollar Bill origami patterns as an example), hexagonal, and even circular, although this last one is the rarest to find patterns for and is primarily used for kirigami. Here's a big note for you – while experimentation and modification are always encouraged in the origami world, there remains an underlying belief to preserve the integrity of the art by *never* cutting or pasting paper. By then it is no longer origami, it is a different art form altogether known as kirigami.

Tools

Once you have developed the feel and touch for folding paper with your hands alone, there are a few tools that you can add to your bag to enhance your experience and designs. Below is a list of common tools and a brief explanation for when and how they are useful.

Bone Folders – The name sounds pretty gnarly and was quite literal in years past, although folding tools today are typically made out of plastic or bamboo rather than bone; partly due to ethical reasons, partly because of demand, and otherwise because the bone eventually dries out and becomes brittle and useless. These are tools to help you fold and crease much more quickly once you have gotten your alignments down, providing you with a nice, crisp crease every time.

You can always use an old or current credit card as a folder, which works nicely, as well as a metal spoon. The bamboo and plastic versions to be bought online or in craft stores usually double as the next tool on the list, tapering at one end.

Picks – These are pointed objects that are really useful for reversing the points of pocketed folds like the sink fold, as well as helping to nestle in some of the more difficult or stubborn crimp folds. Basically you can use anything pointy to your advantage for this tool, as long as you are aware that the pointier the object, the more of a chance you have to poke a hole or tear the paper.

Ballpoint pens that have dried up or run out of ink are useful but they have the tendency to be too pointed. In this case, you can find a bone folder that has one end tapered into a pick as a multi-versed tool, use a small crochet needle that is blunted at the end or the end of a fine paintbrush handle used for watercolors and the like. These tools are also great for wrapping the edges of a finished product around to give them a sufficient curl in patterns such as the petals of some flowers, long animal tails and so on.

Paints, markers, and other crafts – These are enhancers for your completed piece to make them more attractive. Other crafts can include cutting up paper laced doilies and gluing them on, such as a saddle for the horse you've made. You can add sequins, glitter, and more if you so wish. You can also choose to paint or mark up your personally designed prints on a solid-colored paper, even white computer paper, before you begin folding. Just remember, as you will notice when working with other print papers, that it is difficult to tell what parts of the paper will be showing in the final piece and what parts will be hidden between the folds.

Folds

The following folds are commonly seen in intermediate level designs, from the most basic patterns at this stage such as the crane and up throughout more advanced patterns. You may also find more challenging intermediate designs call for advanced folds, so it will do you well to go through them in the next section and familiarize yourself even if you are still at this level. Remember that most patterns requiring complex and compound folds are not ambiguous or raw movements that are supposed to just fit into place. They are set up and supported like scaffolding with pre-creases to help make the large fold more fluid.

Reverse – This is a common fold for the legs, necks, and tails in animal models to create knees and lower legs, feet, and heads as well as kinks and curves for grasses and leaves in plant models. You will usually have a longer, skinny obtuse triangle segment that can open up and looks like a "V" if you look straight on at the cross section. Consider the inside tip of this "V" to be a valley fold and the outside tip to be a mountain fold, which is really representing the long folded edge of the triangle segment.

You can either do a closed reverse fold or an open reverse fold from this position. The closed reverse fold will have you open up the segment and bend a part of it in toward the valley, so that the piece of the segment bending in will turn from a mountain fold (the outside of the "V") to a valley fold.

The open reverse fold is just the backwards version of the closed reverse. At the appropriate position along the triangle segment, open it up and bend the upper portion of it outward so that what was the valley fold of the upper portion has now become a mountain fold.

Squash – This is a fun fold that is commonly seen as a method to shortcut the construction of the water bomb base and the preliminary square base, the latter used in construction of the crane. So you know, the water bomb is simply an inside-out version of the square base, and you can easily use one to get to the other. In order to illustrate the squash fold, which is fun to do, I will take you through the construction steps of the square base.

Take a square piece of paper and line up one corner to an opposite corner, making sure that the edges are aligned so that the remaining to corners are halved exactly with the diagonal fold when you crease it. You have just created a valley fold. Now do the same to the other two opposing corners so that you have two valley folds on the same side of the paper. Keep this second crease you've made folded so that you have an isosceles triangle and a visible crease going from the 90 degree corner to the middle of the long edge.

This is the squash fold part. Now take one 45 degree corner and fold it completely down to the 90 degree corner so that you line up the side edge of the sharper corner with the pre-crease going down the middle. Open this fold back up and, holding the isosceles triangle by the opposite side of the pre-crease, open the other side with the crease you've just made so it looks like an open pocket and bend what was the 45 degree angle open and back down to align with the 90 degree angle. It should look like you've just created a small square lying on top of the overall piece.

Turn the piece over. You should notice the potential for a repeated pattern of what you've just done. On a side note, observing these repeating patterns and how they are formed will advance your skills for knowing what to do next. So then, take the remaining 45 degree corner, open up this flap and – Squash! – bring it down to meet with the bottom 90 degree angle. You have just created a preliminary square base. Congratulations!

Simply as a demonstration, now that you have created a square base, open up the entire paper again to a flattened sheet with all the creases you've made, and turn it inside out. The creases that were valley folds will become mountain folds and vice versa. Pinch the middles of the square sheet sides together so that looking overhead, it appears like an "X" or a "+".

Looking from a side view, it will appear as another isosceles triangle. It should flatten easily so that you have a layered isosceles triangle now. This is a water bomb base. You can go back and forth between the water bomb and square base to observe how they are constructed and familiarize yourself with exactly what you've done. After that, you will have it memorized and creating one thereafter will be a piece of cake.

Petal – These folds are typical for creating wings, ears, leaves and heads in origami, among others. To explain how a petal fold is done, we will start from a square base. This is the next step in creating a crane, in particular.

From your square base, you will need to make three pre-creases. You already have a pre-crease going down the middle from the top closed corner of the square to the bottom open corner. Note that you should have two flaps (a front and a back flap) on either side of this middle pre-crease. Take the front flap of one of the side corners and bend it in toward the middle, lining up the bottom edge of the flap with the middle pre-crease all the way down to the bottom corner. Repeat on the other side with the second front flap.

Turn the piece over. Now the back flaps are your new front flaps. Repeat the same process as you did before. You will know that you have done it right when the piece looks like a kite and all the edges are lined up with each other. Do you see how you have created a horizontal line with your folded flaps at the new side corners of the kite? Fold the top triangle of this kite over one side of the horizontal flaps to make a crease along it, then open up that fold and do the same on the other side. You have just finished creating your three pre-creases for the petal fold.

Open up all the flaps so that your piece resembles the square base again. Now open up the bottom corner of the front square so that it folds up along the horizontal pre-crease. Keep bending this corner backward, and as you do, take your thumbs and tuck the side corners of the front square in toward the middle until they meet together and lay flat. This is the quintessential petal fold. Turn the piece over and repeat the same thing on the other side. Now your piece should look like a four-sided diamond. Great job!

Advanced Info for Experts

When getting into advanced designs, the concentration lies more in the number of pre-creases and layers of folds, possibly smaller sizes of paper for tiny origami, as well as creating more details for a realistic piece. This can include feet for the legs, ears, eyes, and texturized bodies like the scales on a fish or dragon or feathers on a bird.

Paper is chosen particularly with the finished piece in mind that will somehow compliment, enhance or accentuate the design to make it more intriguing and attractive. Tools that are used are sometimes particularly compulsory at this stage because fingers cannot construct the necessary details, although some experts have found ways to use only their natural God-given tools still.

Paper

The choice of paper in advanced origami tends to get quite specialized to really make a piece stand out, although this does not mean that it has to appear exotic. Some thicker grades of paper can be subtle enhancers to an overall design by offering more rounded curves at creases and wider gaps between layers, affecting the way that light plays on the form. These forms of paper come from cardstock, a special range of cardboard paper, something known as VOG from Vietnam that can be found online, and elephant hide paper.

Another quality type of paper used is known as foil paper. This type is a favorite to use for origami insect designs, fish, and elaborate dragons. There are different grades of superiority for this type of paper. You can choose to buy the conventional square sheets of foil paper of one solid color (usually gold, silver, bronze and copper), usually sold in packages at craft stores or online. There is the option to find illustrious foil wrapping paper that you can cut into your own squares, and this way you can find a greater range of pattern options that will make any piece you create look metallic, ornamental, and statuesque. As a matter of fact, you can use any type of wrapping paper for origami, although the thicker types will prove more suitable. This proves to be extremely cost effective, especially since you'll get a whole roll to work with. You can also save yourself some money and make your own foil paper with some aluminum foil sheets, spray glue and a light paper backing.

Tissue origami paper, which is more coarse and stiff than conventional tissue paper, is beautiful for giving your figures a sense of light airiness and delicacy. It folds extremely well but is very unforgiving for mistakes, as is with most foil papers, so you must be gentle and careful when folding. Round the folds to gentle creases and do not use bone folders; your fingers are enough.

Most types of specialized paper will be difficult to find in stores however if you have a local Asian/Oriental gift shop near you, you might have some luck. Your best bet is to find them online, where you can still usually find good deals and your options are extensive.

Tools

Some patterns, such as the Kawasaki swirl rose, actually require the use of tools as opposed to them being optional. In the swirl rose, tweezers or small needle-nose pliers are needed to achieve the tight swirl. Tiny origami is facilitated with the use of a scope or magnifying glass on a stand and tiny, flat, plastic folders and combo picks that are slightly larger than a toothpick.

Pliers – used to achieve twists, tight curls, and pinch thick folds, especially with a heavier-weight grade of paper, for a secure crease. Be sure to use pliers *without teeth*, as the rigid toothed version will make unwanted imprints in the paper.

Tweezers – synonymous uses to the pliers. Sometimes easier to get into tighter spaces. Be careful not to poke through the paper with the pointed tips.

Spray glue – also paper glue. Great for making your own foil paper. Paper glue can be used to secure wavering limbs or other appendages in order to secure the foundation of the three-dimensional figure so that it can stand on its own.

Adds touch ups for a final, polished piece that can be proudly presented as a true work of art.

Furthermore, if you are going to display your completed pieces, you may choose to find interesting bases for them to stand on, which you will have to attach them to in some way. Suggestions for bases include intriguing pieces of driftwood or stones, carved and varnished wood or heavy metallic bases. Try to find one that best compliments your figure. If you are considering to sell your pieces, you may choose to coat them in a thin layer of epoxy that can sometimes be sprayed on (ask around a hardware store or look online), or poured into a bucket that you may dip your figure into with a pair of tongs you don't care much for.

Folds

There are a few more essential fold types to know for advanced techniques, and while they are listed here, words alone would not do justice to their involvement. Therefore it is recommended that you look up the diagrams and steps to execute them with a clear understanding.

Crimp – used to create and detail tails, wings and facilitate joints at limbs in the final stages. In earlier stages, this fold helps to shape and tighten or narrow the body in some way.

Rabbit Ear – narrows the design of the paper and creates a new flap. Similar method to the petal fold in that you must make three pre-creases before completing the full fold.

Sink – used to establish a standing base for a piece or remove rough edges or pointed tips that will not be shown when the figure is complete.

More... – swivel fold, twist fold, stretch folds and sink variants. These are easy enough to find in books and online where diagrams make them much more favorable and approachable to execute.

Once you have gotten a grip on these key folds from beginner level through to the advanced level, you have effectively equipped yourself to approach several different patterns and the rest becomes much easier to tackle. Experiment with different types of paper to see which ones you prefer and what kind of interesting results you get from combining different designs with different paper. You will see that the type and appearance of paper adds a whole new dimension to the figure itself, and some combinations play really well together. Although tools are not an absolute must, once you start getting into the more complex designs you might find that their use will make your life easier. This is especially the case for bone folders if you choose to get into Modular or Golden Venture origami, creating all of those individual modules.

Bases

As you move through the complexity of origami design by trying out different patterns, you'll start to notice further down the road that construction usually happens in three stages: the pre-crease and base-building stage, the figure formation stage and the detail stage. These aren't the official names for the different phases of origami construction. They describe the different primary techniques used in each of the stages that are widely recognized within the origami practice and community.

The real exciting part of trying out new and inventive patterns is discovering different base styles. When you develop an eye for origami folding, you will see common base patterns surface that keep reappearing as they are used for multiple models. Once you see and fold them so many times, you have the base constructions down pat. This is going to make it really easy for you to carve your way through so many more designs. Remembering how the bases are made off-hand will help you understand the way that more complex designs start out and how they achieve what they do. It will speed up your construction and help you keep your edges flush for a sharp and sturdy figure. It will also pave a path for you to pick up from, where you can begin pioneering your own distinctive designs.

In this section you'll learn three of the most common bases used among many origami designs. They will get you started for mastering your pre-crease techniques, employing some of the different folds you've just learned, and practicing to start creating figures in the next chapter.

Fish Base

This base is used for a lot of different – you guessed it! – origami fish designs. It's also used for bird patterns too because it employs a rabbit ear fold that creates a flap ideal for making fins, feathers, wings and ears.

Step 1: Take a square piece of paper, colored side down. Make two pre-creases by valley folding the paper in half: once from one corner to the opposite one, and then again with the other two opposing corners. Open the paper, white side up again. You should have two valley folds that cross each other in the center of the paper, looking like a big "X". These are pre-creases. They are called so because they are made just to create a fold line in the paper without actually keeping the fold (you usually open the fold back up after making it). They also help to make other folds later on in the design, as you will see happen here.

Step 2: Turn your square paper 45 degrees so that it's a diamond shape and a corner is facing you. We'll call this the bottom corner. The others are the side corners and the top corner. From the bottom corner, fold the left side corner in toward the center of the paper so that the bottom left edge of your diamond meets flush with the vertical center line (previous pre-crease). Open the paper up again. Do the same for the right side. These are more pre-creases that will help to make the rabbit ear.

Step 3: Repeat step 2, now starting the left and right folds from the top corner. The top edges should meet flush with the centerline. Open these folds back up again. Notice the symmetry of origami folding here: The top corner and bottom corner pre-creases you've just made should cross each other on each side exactly where the horizontal mid-line pre-crease of your diamond is. Now close these folds again back toward the central line. Your model will look like an upside-down kite shape.

Step 4: This is where the rabbit ear fold happens. Take a good look at the colored triangle flaps on the top part of your figure. There are two pre-creases in each side. The bottom pre-crease is going to mountain fold, and where the two meet on the outer edges, a horizontal valley fold will be made. Start by taking the corner of the left triangle flap that's in the center and lift it upward and further up the central line. The bottom edge of the colored triangle (shortest edge) will want to line up to be flush with the central line, so do it. The rest of the bottom left side that was the white part of the figure will turn over and want to meet flush with the central line as well. It will fold along the left pre-crease made from the bottom corner of your figure. That's really all you have to do, because the pre-creases makes it so easy. Once you have the left bottom edge turned into meet the central line, the little rabbit earflap will form from the colored triangle as you continue to fold it up along the central line. A lot of visualization for a seamless move.

Step 5: Repeat step 4 for the right side. Congratulations, you've made your first fish base!

Square Base

This and the water bomb base (following) are opposite twins of each other. What it means you can turn one inside out and it will become the other. This poses somewhat of a versatile choice for you, because if you like the construction method of one base over the other, you can stick to that one and just turn the figure inside-out when you need to use the other.

The square base makes use of the squash fold and sets up the process for making a wide range of animal origami, most popular of which is the paper crane, which you will learn how to make in the next chapter. It's a good idea to have a bunch of papers in front of you to practice while reading this section and the next one.

Step 1: Start with a square piece of paper, colored side down, and turn it 45 degrees so that a corner is facing you and it looks like a diamond. Valley fold the top half of the diamond down to the bottom half, making sure the corners and edges line up perfectly.

Step 2: Now halve this downward facing triangle by making a vertical valley fold from the bottom corner. Bring the right topside corner over to meet with the left. Again, match everything up so that it's flush.

Step 3: Here comes the squash fold. Hold your piece in place. From the longest edge of this new triangle on the bottom left, take a finger and lift the topmost flap of paper. The top left corner of the triangle will start to open up, and when it does, bring it opened and press flat so that it meets the bottom corner perfectly. Your figure should look like a smaller, colored, diamond-shaped square with a downward pointing triangle flap coming off of the top left edge of the diamond. Got that squared away? Of course you do!

Step 4: Keep your figure oriented as it is and flip it over to the other side now. That triangle flap that was on the left side will now be on the right. You're going to squash fold this one the same way that you did the first. The top right corner of your piece will open up and a pocket is made. Fold the pocket down so that the triangle flap squashes into a square or diamond, matching the edges of the one you made on the other side – the top right corner will open up to meet the bottom corner. You now have a compact square base, ready to get wild with any number of animal designs.

Water bomb Base

Well, since this is the opposite twin of the square base, things will be different but similar. First off, like it was mentioned, you could just take your square base, open the flaps up from the bottom corner and find the middle (inside of the top corner), then push that middle inside out and re-crease the folds in the new way. The water bomb base will look like an upward-pointing right triangle or pyramid whose bottom opens up to pockets.

Then again, it would be great just to show you so you can do it and see for yourself. Remember how the square base started with the square paper turned like a diamond? The water bomb's beginning orientation will remain square.

Step 1: Take a square piece of paper, colored side down, and fold the top half down to meet the corners and edges of the bottom half in the shape of a rectangle. Make sure that they line up perfectly first, then crease the fold.

Step 2: Halve your rectangular figure by folding the left side over the right side. Again, match up the corners and edges first, then make a neat crease.

Step 3: From the bottom right corner of this compact square you've created, open just the top flap. Another squash fold is coming, can you feel it? This square is going to squash into a pyramid-shaped triangle. Bring the bottom right corner of the square over to the left side and it will make a mountain fold to halve this corner when you squash it. What *was* the top right corner of the square will open up and become the vertical midline of your pyramid. The bottom right corner of the second flap from the top will stay at the right side, but it will also mountain fold in half. That's the squash.

Step 4: Keeping the same top-and-bottom orientation of your figure, flip it over and repeat the squash fold for the backside. When completed, you should have a uniform, compacted pyramid shape whose bottom opens up to reveal pockets. This is the water bomb base. Good Job!

You now have a great grasp on the fundamentals of origami folding. You know the purpose of pre-creases and how to make them, you've executed some pretty amazing intermediate folds that you've just learned, and now you have the practice of creating three origami bases to skyrocket your adventures into all different kinds of designs. Are you ready for some hands-on experience? Turn to the next chapter and tuck your fingers into some classic, some functional, and some wild origami designs.

Sandra Gifford

Origami Designs

In this chapter you are going to get some real hands-on training in making origami with various patterns. The chapter after this one is going to detail several origami books that you can look into which will provide many, many more patterns for you to practice and add to the library of designs that you are able to create. You will find in these recommended books, as it has already been described, that most use the pictorial Yoshizawa-Randlett system for illustrating the steps of how to make any particular design.

When you become more advanced and start getting into detail work, some of these books do not use the Yoshizawa-Randlett system and instead simply show pictures of completed designs. Being at such an advanced level, you are expected to be able to interpret which kinds of folds and techniques have been employed so that you may gain further insight as to how you can apply them to make your designs more interesting as well as create more complicated models.

This is why if you intend to pursue origami to a higher degree, it is so important that you learn the very foundation of common and sometimes uncommon folds and bases. In doing so, you will be able to take a look at an already completed model of an origami piece that you are unfamiliar with and identify what methods have been used to create its basic structure. From there, it will require your skills of observation and interpretation to unravel the deeper secrets of the origami masters. A great deal of origami making in these higher levels involves experimentation as well. Advanced folders didn't get to where they are without making mistakes! So you should not be afraid to go out on a limb and try new things with your paper folding skills either. You may just surprise yourself!

In this particular book and chapter, you will learn how to make some of the most common origami models in a step by step process. Each will be categorized from beginner to intermediate and advanced. You should know that truly advanced models of origami often take over 100 steps to complete. It is a time consuming hobby, yet it feels so rewarding and awe-inspiring once you finish a model of your own creation. That being said, the advanced level designs outlined here are relative to an introductory level origami enthusiast. They may pale in comparison to how difficult and complicated some original designs of origami can truly get, however they will present a stimulating challenge to those who are just starting out.

In addition to that, the instructional steps for the origami designs provided in this book will be outlined in clear-cut, straightforward text. It will not be using illustrations or the Yoshizawa-Randlett system to walk you through the folding process. This may seem like a slight disadvantage for you visual learners, in which case it is recommended that you attempt to seek out some illustrative instructions online to compliment the text instructions for any particular model in this book. The upshot of working with text instructions in origami is that they are going to allow you to get familiar with the names of the common folds and base constructions very quickly. You will also greatly develop the internal visual mind for imagining how a fold should look.

As an example, the way that athletes fine-hone their performance, especially Olympian athletes, is by visualizing every move and method of their technique before actually going out and doing it. This helps to train their focus, but also they are using their concentration to embody the move from the inside out, creating a complete and thorough understanding for themselves.

You can use your concentration and knowledge and apply it to *anything* in the same way to get better results. In origami, you can develop the intimate knowledge of what folds look like and how they are done easily so someone may just say "reverse fold" and in your mind you will already know the look and feel of it with the snap of a finger. Applying yourself in such a way greatly improves your speed and skill in origami so that you make propel yourself into taking on more creative and challenging designs.

Through visual depictions, a person could be looking at the steps to create a base over and over again for several different models and not make the connection to shortcut these steps since they keep creating the same initial formation. Through textual descriptions, the moment that you see the phrase "create a square base", you will be able to refer to the squash fold details in the previous section, either physically or through memory, and instantly know the four steps it takes to form this base. This method will save you time and reinforce your fundamental knowledge of origami construction and the craft at large.

Beginner: Boats, Hats and Boxes

These designs use mountain and valley folds for the most part. Some are ornamental such as the boat and hat, while the box can be used for little gifts to give to a friend or relative, or serve as a candy dish.

Boat

Let's go for a sailing trip! This one is simple and fun, great for an ornament on the desk or bed stand. Kids will love this one too.

Step 1: Take a square piece of paper, color side up, and make a valley fold from one corner to another to divide the paper into half (two triangles). Open the paperback up and flip it over so that the white (non-color, or back) side is facing up.

Step 2: Valley fold the paper in half to make a rectangle, making sure the edges and corners meet. Open the paper back up. Now do the same for the other two edges. Open up the paper again. Your square paper should now be divided into four smaller squares with a diagonal fold bisecting two of them.

Step 3: For the two smaller squares that are not bisected by the diagonal fold, valley fold them from the outer corners into the center of the paper (which you can find by where the preliminary folds intersect). The corners should just meet tip to tip in the center. Now it will look like two colored triangles mirroring each other at the apex.

Step 4: Bend the opposing outer corners of the white squares with the diagonal centerfold in toward each other. As you bring the corners together, the white squares will fold inward along the diagonal fold and these folded edges will meet together in the middle, right up to the corners.

These are the sails. You now have a very basic-looking sailboat.

Step 5: You're going to crimp one of the sails to make it a bit shorter than the other. Valley fold one of the sails down to meet corners with the bottom boat part of the colored paper. Now, a little further down from where you have created this fold at the junction of the boat and sail, make a parallel horizontal fold in the sail back upward again so that it is shorter than the other sail.

Step 6: To complete the crimp, bring the folded sail up straight again, open the flap of the boat on that side, and fold the sail down and into this opened flap. The top corner of the sail and the bottom corner of the boat should meet. Now at the second fold you made in the sail, fold it upward again. Close the boat flap. Both sails should be "sitting inside" the boat now, one shorter than the other.

Step 7: Take the bottom corner of the boat and fold it backward so that it meets the middle of the horizontal edge of the colored paper boat part. Make a good crease here. This is the platform to help the sailboat stand up. Congratulations, you've done it!

Samurai Hat

This is a classic origami pattern that is very popular, fun, and easy to do. They are mostly ornamental, but if you'd like to get creative, you can use bobby pins, paper clips, or a large needle and string to attach them to your head as a funny party favor. Depending on the size of paper you use, you could get closer to an actual hat.

Step 1: Take a square piece of paper, color side facing down, and valley fold it in half diagonally, meeting up the edges and corners together. Orient the paper so that the long edge is on top and the 90 degree angle of the triangle you've made is pointing toward you.

Step 2: Take the corners of the long edge of the triangle and valley fold these to meet together at the bottom corner of the triangle. The edges should line up in the middle.

Step 3: Make a horizontal valley fold in the middle of these triangle flaps. The corners that you had brought down to the bottom will now fold up to meet each other at the top corner.

Step 4: Now, keeping those folds as is, take the corner of each of these flaps, one at a time, and make an angled valley fold so that the corner is pointing out to the side. These are the "horns" of the helmet. The origin of this fold will start from the inside center corner you have created by folding the flaps upward. The degree of the angle for the fold you make to point the corners out at each side is up to you. Traditionally, once folded, the top edge of these "horns" is horizontal.

Step 5: You have two triangular flaps as the bottom half of your overall square-shaped paper. Take the corner of this front flap and make a horizontal valley fold upward. Where you make this fold is somewhat arbitrary, up to you. The corner of the flap will align with the center "line", and is good to place right in the middle of the upper "triangle" of your overall piece.

Step 6: Making the previous fold should leave you some space between it and the central horizontal fold made by the "horned" flaps. Valley fold this strip upward, right at the central horizontal fold. This is the brim of the samurai hat or helmet. Flip your piece over.

Step 7: Repeat step 6 for this back bottom flap. Now you have a full-brimmed hat. Flip the piece over again.

Step 8: You have your fully decked out samurai hat, now all that's left to do is open it up. From the bottom long edge that would sit on the head, stick your finger between the front and back brims and open the hat up to become 3D and soften the creases of the top edges. You can also curl the brim a bit to give it more shape. Alright, good job! Time to party!

Box 1

Just like the Cat in the Hat has Thing 1 and Thing 2 that come in boxes, we are going to make box 1 and box 2 here. They're great for keeping *things*, jewelry, buttons, pins, and other assorted small items in. They can be used for gift giving as well as candy or snack dishes to be left out for guests, friends, family and yourself. If you have or know children that you could teach these patterns to, they make for great quality time spent together around the holidays or whenever!

Step 1: Take a square piece of paper with the color side down and valley fold it in half vertically to make a rectangle. Match up the edges and corners together. Open the paper back up. Valley fold it in half again, horizontally this time to make another rectangle. Open the paper back up.

Step 2: Valley fold each of the corners into the middle so that they meet at where the center folds intersect. You should have a colored square tipped on its corner, or a "squared diamond" shape. Turn your piece 45 degrees so that you're looking at a square now.

Step 3: Make a note of where the central horizontal line of this square is. You're going to make two horizontal valley folds, above and below this central horizontal line. The top and bottom edges of the square will meet in the middle. Crease these folds, then open them back up.

Step 4: Open the top and bottom triangular flaps of your square. Now make a complete vertical valley fold on each of the sides of your piece. The edges of the colored triangles will meet together vertically in the center. You should now have a strip of paper that has two colored vertical strips and two white "squared diamond" shapes at the top and bottom.

Step 5: Make a note of the bottom edges of the white squared diamond that is at the top of the strip of paper. Make a valley fold to the right, using the right bottom edge of this white squared diamond as a guide. The fold will go through a bit of the colored part of the left vertical strip. Open this fold up, then repeat for the left side. Open up this second fold.

Step 6: Repeat step 5 for the white squared diamond at the bottom of the strip. This time the top edges of the squared diamond will serve as a guideline for the valley folds.

Step 7: Make a note of where these folds you have just made end at the edges of the colored strip portions of the paper. These are going to be the corners of the open part of the box. Read the following instructions carefully and completely before making your next move. Take the vertical strips of colored paper from where they meet in the middle and open them up so that the central edges are standing up. These are two of the walls of your box. Push the top and bottom sections of the paper containing the squared diamonds up so that the folds you have made through the colored strips collapse into each other. What you're looking at here are the walls of the box on your left and right, with the bottom corners of the squared diamonds touching the middle of the edges of your top and bottom walls.

Step 8: Fold the squared diamond flaps into the box. Make a mountain fold along the top edge of the box wall and a horizontal valley fold that bisects the squared diamonds. Tuck the flaps in so that everything is flat against the walls and bottom of the box. Remember how your piece looked at the end of step 2? That's how the inside of the bottom of the box should look now, except your square has walls now! That's how you do "origami box 1". If you'd like a lid for your box, simply repeat steps 1 through 8 and then fit one box inside the other.

Intermediate: Canoes, Boxes and Cranes

These origami designs will introduce a few more tricks to diversify your folding palette. The canoe can actually float on water, although some types of paper work better than others. Basic origami paper does nicely. It will show you an inside out, turning method that can be applied for other designs and is seen in the common sink fold.

The box you will see here is a 3D, fully enclosed box. It will introduce a tuck-in method to you that fortifies some origami designs and relates to modular origami in how the modules connect to each other.

The classic paper crane design has already been half constructed for you through the description of the folds in the previous chapter! To help you memorize these steps they will be repeated fully here. Both the crane design and the 3D box will get you to employ a fun trick of some 3D models that requires you to blow into them to get the full shape. Let's begin!

Canoe

This is a great interactive design that is really fun to make and provides plenty of entertainment after its completion, too! You can float it on water or use it for a candy/snack dish as well. With a large enough sized paper, you could serve hors d'oeuvres on them at get-togethers and parties.

It will probably do you good to know that since you are going to be turning this piece inside-out at the end, the side of the paper that is face-down when you start will be the inside of the canoe at the end. That means that if you start with the colored side down, the inside will be colored and the outside will be while. Vice versa, if you start with the colored side up then the inside of your canoe will be white. It's up to you, but for the sake of these instructions we will start with the colored side down.

Step 1: Begin with a square piece of paper, colored side down. Make a vertical valley fold in the center of the paper by matching up the corners and edges together. Open the paper back up.

Step 2: Now half the two rectangles you've just made by valley folding each vertical edge of your paper into the centerfold you made in step one.

Step 3: You are going to fold four triangles, one for each corner. At the top of the paper, take a corner and valley fold it into the centerline so that the top edge is flush with it. Do the same for the other three corners.

Step 4: You should now have something of an upright, six-sided diamond shape. From the topmost corner to the middle of the left vertical edge of your piece, make a valley fold and crease it. The corner of this tiny flap that folds in will almost touch the central line, but not quite. Repeat for the other three sides. The top and bottom flaps of these folds on one particular side will meet together in the middle of the vertical edge or should, but it's not crucial that you get it perfect. If they overlap each other a little bit, that's ok.

Step 5: You should now have a four-sided, diamond-shaped piece. Make two valley folds, one for each side, by bringing the side corners (the wider corners of the diamond) in to meet each other at the central line. The folds should be parallel with the central line and the tips of the side corners should just touch in the middle of the piece. You have just finished creating the walls of the boat that will fortify its shape for happy cruising.

Step 6: Get ready for the magic. This central line of your piece is where all the action is going to happen. Hold the piece vertically in your hands. Place your thumbs on the top of each side and the rest of your fingers along each side of the central line. Bend the piece along the central line so that the middle mountain folds toward you. Use your thumbs to gently grab these pockets from the inside. Now use the rest of your fingers from the back to push up while your thumbs turn the pockets you've inserted them into inside out. Your canoe will most easily pop into shape by reversing the four side corners of your piece. Zippo-presto! You're ready for lazy river cruising or party-mix munching, enjoy!

Box 2

And now, Thing 2 comes out of the box. Or, switch that, we're going to put an origami lock on this thing in a box. This design is also known as the origami balloon. If you make a bunch of these you can get creative with them as building blocks. Or, if you're feeling really creative and decorative and you can find the patience to manage it, you can take a string of Christmas lights and poke the light bulb portion into the hole of these boxes that you will use to blow them up. It'd be best to use medium to large-sized paper for that purpose. And voila, you have a lit string of Chinese lanterns!

Step 1: You're going to create a water bomb base here. Start with a square piece of paper with the colored side face down. Half the paper by creating a horizontal valley fold, making sure the edges and corners line up to make a rectangle.

Step 2: Half your rectangle piece by making a vertical valley fold, folding the left side over the right. You should now have a square piece.

Step 3: You're going to do a squash fold here so that the top square flap you've just folded becomes a large triangle. The vertical right edge of your square will become the bottom long edge of the triangle. Take the very top flap of paper from the bottom right corner and insert your finger to open it up. As you do, bring that top corner over to the left and squash the entire square flap. The top edge of the square now becomes the vertical midline of the triangle. Flip the piece over and squash the other side to meet the bottom corner of the first triangle you created. All of the sides should be flush with each other. Congratulations, you've just finished your water bomb base, but you're not done yet!

Step 4: You're going to create two valley folds here, one on each side of the triangle. Bring the bottom corners of the top flaps of your water bomb base up to meet at the top corner. What were the bottom edges of these flaps will meet flush at the centerline. Flip your piece over and repeat on the same side. For the integrity of these instructions and to avoid confusion, be sure to maintain the top and bottom orientation of your piece as you flip over from one side to the other.

Step 5: Bring in the side corners of the top flaps by making a vertical valley fold on each side. The tips of the corners should meet in the middle of the piece at the centerline. Flip the piece over and repeat for the other side.

Step 6: Make a horizontal valley fold downward with the tips of the flaps at the top of your piece. The top edges of the flaps should meet flush with the edges of the other folds you made in step 5. Flip your piece over and repeat for the other side.

Step 7: Here comes the tuck-in part. First you're going to make a pre-crease valley fold for each of the flaps you just folded in step 6. Fold the corners of these flaps toward the sides of your piece, right along where the flush edges described in step 6 meet. Open these folds up again. Now take your finger and open up the pocket of the fold you made in step 5. Tuck the flap of the pre-creased part you just made into this pocket. Repeat this three more times for the other flaps.

Step 8: Your overall piece should resemble an upright, six-sided diamond shape. Consider it to be a square with a triangle sitting on the top and bottom of it. Make a horizontal, valley fold pre-crease where these triangles would meet the square (one for the top and one for the bottom). Unfold what you've just done.

Step 9: Now for the fun part. You have already created your box, you just need to blow it up! The hole is located at the bottommost corner of this six-sided diamond you have. Simply hold the piece up to your mouth lightly with your fingers. It may help to slip an index finger in between the side flaps to open it up a little. Now put the bottom tip to your lips and blow into the box like you are blowing into a balloon. Does that thing just puff right up or what?

You may have to lightly use your fingers to finish bringing the box into its full shape. This gentle detail work is great practice for your fingers and concentration. It's the kind of careful, meticulous skill to develop that will add detail to your future designs, crafting and shaping them in ways that you see fit to add interest to the overall piece.

Remember now that the hole you just used to blow the box up is the same one into which you can insert the bulb of a string of Christmas lights. It may not look like it's possible, but trust me, it is. You will have to be a little patient and very gentle to get it to fit in, as well as do some more finger tinkering to reshape the box after you've inserted the bulb. Also, for safety's sake, make sure the box fits up around the plastic casing of the bulb. Do not leave the paper touching the bulb itself.

Crane

The classic paper crane that gets so much prestige is finally here at your fingertips. It's fun and challenging enough for adults and kids alike. The crane pattern employs some more folds you've read about in the previous section that we'll go over again, including the petal fold and reverse fold. It all begins with a square base. Once you move on from there, there's no telling how many paper cranes will fill and delight your life with a lofty, carefree attitude.

Step 1: Start with a square piece of paper, colored side down, and turn it 45 degrees so that a corner is facing you and it looks like a diamond. Valley fold the top half of the diamond down to the bottom half, making sure the corners and edges line up perfectly.

Step 2: Now halve this downward facing triangle by making a vertical valley fold from the bottom corner. Bring the right topside corner over to meet with the left. Again, match everything up so that it's flush.

Step 3: Here comes the squash fold. Hold your piece in place. From the longest edge of this new triangle on the bottom left, take a finger and lift the topmost flap of paper. The top left corner of the triangle will start to open up, and when it does, bring it opened and press flat so that it meets the bottom corner perfectly. Your figure should look like a smaller, colored, diamond-shaped square with a downward pointing triangle flap coming off of the top left edge of the diamond.

Step 4: Keep your figure oriented as it is and flip it over to the other side now. That triangle flap that was on the left side will now be on the right. You're going to squash fold this one the same way that you did the first. The top right corner of your piece will open up and a pocket is made. Fold the pocket down so that the triangle flap squashes into a square or diamond, matching the edges of the one you made on the other side – the top right corner will open up to meet the bottom corner. Boom. Square base. Keep your piece oriented so that the bottom corner pointing toward you is the one that opens up from the inside.

Step 5: You're going to set up for a petal fold here, and to do that you need to make three pre-creases to facilitate it's execution. Start by taking the top flap of the left side corner and make a valley fold that starts from the bottom corner and goes to the midpoint of the top left edge of your diamond (square). You can achieve this by folding over the left top flap and making its bottom edge flush with the vertical centerline of your square base. Now fold the right top flap in toward the center so that its bottom edge lines right up with the bottom edge of the left top flap. Do you see the pyramid-shaped triangle sitting on top of the flaps you've just folded? Valley fold this pyramid downward at the horizontal edge of where the flaps meet. Lightly crease the fold. Now open up all three folds you've just made so you're looking at a square base again.

Step 6: Petal fold time. Take the bottom corner of the topmost diamond flap and insert your finger underneath it to lift the flap upward. The flap will valley fold along the top horizontal pre-crease you've made. The angled pre-creases originating from the bottom corner of the top flap will mountain fold. The bottom edges of the topmost flap for your square base are going to open up, flattening out the folds of the square base's side corners, and all meet together in the vertical centerline of the piece. Petal fold complete.

Step 7: Flip your piece over and repeat steps 5 and 6 to make a petal fold for the backside. Your piece should look like a skinny, four-sided diamond now standing upright.

The left and right flaps on the bottom half of the diamond are separated from each other at the centerline. Each side has a top and bottom flap to it (front and back of the piece). On the left flap, from the bottom corner, make another fold just as you did for the pre-crease of the petal fold. Fold the top flap in toward the centerline so that its bottom edge meets flush with the center edge. The fold will end on the top edge of the left side, although it will be below the midpoint of that edge. You want it this way.

Step 8: Repeat step 7 for the top flap of the right side. Flip your piece over. Repeat step 7 again for the back flaps of both the left and right. Remember that the fold originates from the bottom corner. What you may be feeling in your fingers with this step 7 move for all sides is what happens with multiple folds: the paper gets thicker, making it harder to fold and line up correctly. Don't worry if it's not perfect, just keep practicing, and remember the tips given earlier in the book to get a great fold every time. Building up this delicate, skinny thickness in the crane model is partly what makes it a more challenging design to create, however it makes such a great, rewarding milestone once you've completed one.

Step 9: You've just created the neck and tail of your crane with these skinny, sharp limbs in the bottom half of your piece. The top half contains the wings and body, but in order to get them to open up, you're going to have to create some reverse folds in the neck and tail. Find the point at which the center divide begins in the bottom of your piece. It will be near the middle. Take the complete left "limb" and make a valley fold. It will start from the point you've found near the center and go at a downward angle of 45 degrees. Unfold what you've just done.

Now from the outside edge of this left limb, insert your fingers to open it up. Bring the bottom corner or tip of the limb and reverse it: the central valley fold in the opening your fingers made will turn inside out, becoming a mountain fold as you bring the tip of your limb up to the top half of your piece, folding at the pre-crease you've just made. The whole limb from the pre-crease will have reverse folded to tuck up in between the front and back flaps of the top half of your piece.

Step 10: Repeat step 9 for the right side. This is the tail.

Step 11: Create another reverse fold on the left upturned limb. This is the neck, and your bird needs a head! From the tip of the "neck" down about a quarter to a half of the length of the limb that's showing, make a valley fold at a 45 degree angle upward to the left. Unfold this pre-crease. Open up your limb again from the inside edge and push the middle down from the top corner. The limb will fold into itself again, pointing to the left horizontally. There you have it, your crane's head! At the actual reverse fold, the neck part will overlap the head part, confirming that your limb has folded inside itself. This is the nature of the reverse fold.

Step 12: You have the head, neck and tail of your crane, but do you remember which are the wings? The central front and back flaps of your piece! Pull them gently apart and down to each side. The only thing left for you to do is to fill out the body.

Step 13: From where your crane's bottom is located, between where the neck and tail have been reverse folded, there is a small hole in the middle that serves as a cavity to the body. As you gently pull your crane's wings out to the sides, put your mouth up to this hole and blow into it. You're looking at a full-bodied crane, now!

You can use this design as a decoration around the home or office, as a thoughtful little gift to brighten someone's day, or you can create a bunch of cranes and draw strings up through them to create a fun mobile.

Advanced: Seahorse

The seahorse design uses a lot of reverse folds as well as many crimp folds to achieve its shape. After you are finished with it, you are going to feel like a reverse, crimp fold master! It will certainly give you plenty of practice to skillfully develop these techniques. The seahorse pattern begins with a fish base, so let's start there.

Step 1: Take a square piece of paper, colored side down. Make two pre-creases by valley folding the paper in half: once from one corner to the opposite one, and then again with the other two opposing corners. Open the paper, white side up again. You should have two valley folds that cross each other in the center of the paper, looking like a big "X". These are pre-creases.

Step 2: Turn your square paper 45 degrees so that it's a diamond shape and a corner is facing you. We'll call this the bottom corner. The others are the side corners and the top corner. From the bottom corner, fold the left side corner in toward the center of the paper so that the bottom left edge of your diamond meets flush with the vertical center line (previous pre-crease). Open the paper up again. Do the same for the right side. These are more pre-creases that will help to make the rabbit ear.

Step 3: Repeat step 2, now starting the left and right folds from the top corner. The top edges should meet flush with the centerline. Open these folds back up again. Notice the symmetry of origami folding here: The top corner and bottom corner pre-creases you've just made should cross each other on each side exactly where the horizontal mid-line pre-crease of your diamond is. Now close these folds again back toward the central line. Your model will look like an upside-down kite shape.

Step 4: This is where the rabbit ear fold happens. Take a good look at the colored triangle flaps on the top part of your figure. There are two pre-creases in each side. The bottom pre-crease is going to mountain fold, and where the two meet on the outer edges, a horizontal valley fold will be made. Start by taking the corner of the left triangle flap that's in the center and lift it upward and further up the central line. The bottom edge of the colored triangle (shortest edge) will want to line up to be flush with the central line, so do it. The rest of the bottom left side that was the white part of the figure will turn over and want to meet flush with the central line as well. It will fold along the left pre-crease made from the bottom corner of your figure. Once you have the left bottom edge turned into meet the central line, the little rabbit earflap will form from the colored triangle as you continue to fold it up along the central line.

Step 5: Repeat step 4 for the right side.

Step 6: Orient your fish base so that the rabbit earflaps are pointing downward. Make a mountain fold from the central line of your base. You are basically halving the base so that you have a downward facing rabbit ear flap on each side. Orient your halved fish base so that the side corner is facing to the left. The right side of your piece should be a completely vertical edge.

Step 7: Take the rabbit earflap and valley fold it upward at an angle. The fold itself should start from the left side corner and go to the right at a downward angle, about 20 to 30 degrees below the horizontal line of the flap. Your rabbit earflap should be pointing upward now and out to the right. This is going to be the fin of the seahorse.

Step 8: Create a reverse fold near the tip of the fin on the right side. To do this, simply make a valley fold near the tip that is perpendicular with the top edge of the rabbit earflap. Open this fold you just made. Open up the fin from the right edge and tuck the tip of the rabbit ear fold *into* the fin where you made the pre-crease for the reverse fold. Tuck it completely so that what was the top edge of the tip goes from a mountain fold to a valley fold and fits right in with the mountain fold of the rest of the fin. Remember this move, since you'll be doing the same for the tip of the head to make the nose.

Step 9: Flip your piece over and repeat steps 7 and 8 for the other side. Your sea horse's fins are now complete. Flip your piece back over so that the side corner of your fish base is pointing to the left again.

Step 10: From the bottom corner, make an angled valley fold with the top flap of your piece that goes all the way across to the top left edge of your fish base. When you make this fold, the bottom left edge of the top flap will fold over to face the right, dividing the bottom corner, however it will not reach all the way to meet the right edge. Make the fold so that somewhere between half to a little less of the right edge is still showing behind the width of the fold you've made. Flip your piece over and repeat this process for the other side. Flip your piece back once more after you've done this.

Step 11: Reverse fold to create the neck. To do this, make a valley fold pre-crease starting from the left bottom edge of the piece, about one-sixth the length of the entire bottom left edge, or about one-half inch if you are using a medium-sized paper. The fold should be a little wider than being parallel with the top left edge of your piece, meaning that it will be at less of an angle and the top right vertical side of the part you're folding will be longer than the bottom left.

Straighten the pre-crease fold back again. Open your fish base up from the left side and reverse fold the top part of it at the pre-crease you just made.

Step 12: Reverse fold to create the head. To do this, from the top corner that is pointing to the right, find the next top corner to the left of it where the angle of the top edges changes. Make a pre-crease valley fold here that is perpendicular to the topmost edge nearest the endpoint corner. Once you've made the pre-crease, undo it, open up the "neck" from the right side edge (it may help to open up the entire piece) and reverse fold the top section at the pre-crease to overlap the neck. Now you have a seahorse head that should be facing toward the left.

Step 13: Remember what you did for the fins in step 8? You're going to do the same here for the tip of the head to blunt the nose. Make a pre-crease fold that is perpendicular with the bottom edge of the head a little ways from the tip (about a quarter to a half inch with a medium-sized paper). Open up the head from the bottom edge and tuck the tip up into it at the pre-crease you made, making sure that it folds up neatly into the top edge (mountain fold) of the head.

Step 14: You are going to do a parallel or "even" crimp here on the head. You will make two pre-creases. Valley fold the first one, closest to the neck, a little ways away from where the head overlaps with the neck. Make the fold perpendicular with the bottom edge of the head. About an eighth of an inch further out from that pre-crease, make another one that is parallel with it. Now open up the head from the bottom edge completely. The first pre-crease nearest the neck will become a mountain fold and the pre-crease further out from it will become a valley fold. Close the head again at the mountain fold from the top edge with your crimp in place.

Step 15: This is the super crimp stage that will finalize the design of your seahorse. It's going to employ five "v" shaped crimps down the length of your piece at certain points. Once you get the hang of one, you'll know what to do with the others, so the process will described once and then you will be given the locations to do the other four crimps. These crimps are going to cause your seahorse to look straight forward instead of slightly upwards as it is now, and the other four are going to create the sections of the tail and will curl the lower part of the body in toward the left side.

The "v" crimp entails making two pre-creases, just like you did for the parallel crimp. The only difference is the shape. The "v's" will actually be on their side to look like so: ">". The points where the two pre-creases meet for each crimp will be on the right edge of your seahorse. The distance between the pre-creases as they fold across to the left edge will diminish as you go down the length of the tail because it gets skinnier. Therefore, now that you know the basic shape and orientation of the crimps, you can experiment to get the desired effect.

Make a crimp above the fin, starting at the right edge a little above the top of the fin. The top pre-crease can be a little higher than a perpendicular line with the left edge while the bottom pre-crease can be a little lower than it. After making these pre-creases, open up your seahorse from the left edge. For this and each one of the following crimps, the top pre-crease will become a mountain fold and the bottom pre-crease will become a valley fold *for both sides of the seahorse*. The crimp fold is a bit like the reverse fold in this way, in that the figure will fold over itself on both sides to some degree.

For the four remaining "v" crimps, start from the right edge and consider that they should be spaced out equally along the length of the tail in order to create proportionate sections. That being said, if you're using a medium-sized paper, the tip of the "v's" along the right edge of the seahorse may be about one half inch apart, starting from below the fin. When making the pre-creases, the bottom one will be perpendicular with the left edge of the tail and the top one will be angled up some. Again, once you've made the pre-creases and straightened out the tail again, you'll get the crimp effect by folding the top pre-down over the bottom one (the bottom one will become a valley fold).

Congratulations, You've done it! A great challenge, I'm sure, but well worth it. Keep practicing and experimenting with the detail folds. If you felt that you were able to handle that one ok, try making your seahorse 3D by curling in the edges of the left side and the bottom edges of the head. Have fun!

Design Books

This section is simply a quick reference guide to some of the authors and titans in the origami world that have helped hundreds of thousands of people become inspired, explore new realms, advance their techniques, and even learn how to invent their own designs through understanding the geometric principals of origami construction.

Origami Omnibus by Kunihiko Kasahara – This is a great book from a Japanese master that is designed for beginners to intermediate levels with over 250 designs to work from. It is one to elevate your folding soul and keep coming back to for references.

Origami Rings and Wreaths and **Unit Polyhedron Origami** by Tomoko Fuse – Design books for the Modular enthusiast. The first book teaches you how to make several modulated constructions for use as jewelry and decorations in your home or office, also including some more festive holiday designs. The second book has many different designs for modulated shapes that cater to all levels of origami goers and each design includes a star rating of one to three to indicate the difficulty level.

Origami Design Secrets by Robert Lang – This book is a must have for anyone who is looking to advance their craft and especially if they wish to create their own designs. It contains over 500 pages of designs for lower intermediate to advanced levels and several "scientific" folding methods that instruct on how to conceptualize and execute your own personal origami design.

Origami Tessellations: Awe-inspiring Geometric Designs by Eric Gjerde – Here is the introductory book on Tessellation that takes you through the gritty bits and pieces of every aspect of this art form, from the size and type of paper to use to a number of folds seen and used in Tessellation to intricate patterns that can be emulated on skill levels from the beginner to the proficient.

The books here are just a drop in the ocean relevant to what is available out there in search of all different kinds of designs and furthering your knowledge about the practice and facets of origami itself. Consider what types of figures and styles that have been introduced to you through this book really speak to you and inspire your drive to get out there and get started. It is that drive that will help nurture and hone your skills.

Sandra Gifford

Conclusion

The beautiful art of origami has something to offer for everyone. It proposes a unique perspective of how to take a single, uniform and seemingly plain thing such as a sheet of paper and really twist, turn and contort it into a variety of wondrous things. Origami possesses the versatility to go outside its own proverbial paper box and use multiple sheets of folded paper into modules to make a grander composite design. It can stay cool and dry, happy being folded in on itself in the usual way or take a chance to get wet and assume a whole new look.

There is nothing to be intimidated about when it comes to origami. There are multitudes of resources out there along with this book that break down the mystery into easy-to-understand, step-by-step explanations and diagrams so that you can see and comprehend it from every angle. The only thing that origami can't teach is patience. Oh wait! No, it does that too! If you have enough interest to learn how such a mobile, adaptable art transforms the simple and dull into any number of stirring and fun things, it will carry you through learning the patience too that goes hand in hand with achieving this.

Remember that you are stepping into a well-established, international world of paper folding with a rich history and followers from all over the world. There are groups and organizations dedicated to origami, and if you ever get the chance to attend one of their conventions, you will see first-hand just what all of the enthusiasm is about. Good luck, I hope that you have found something that really grabs you within this book and sends you off on paper wings to exploring more about it.

Thank you for purchasing this book.